JER Rabe
Rabe, Tish
Have no fear! Halloween is
  here!

$12.99
ocn925410834

First edition.

Learning to Read, Step by Step!

Ready to Read   Preschool–Kindergarten
• big type and easy words • rhyme and rhythm • picture clues
For children who know the alphabet and are eager to
begin reading.

Reading with Help   Preschool–Grade 1
• basic vocabulary • short sentences • simple stories
For children who recognize familiar words and sound out
new words with help.

Reading on Your Own   Grades 1–3
• engaging characters • easy-to-follow plots • popular topics
For children who are ready to read on their own.

Reading Paragraphs   Grades 2–3
• challenging vocabulary • short paragraphs • exciting stories
For newly independent readers who read simple sentences
with confidence.

Ready for Chapters   Grades 2–4
• chapters • longer paragraphs • full-color art
For children who want to take the plunge into chapter books
but still like colorful pictures.

STEP INTO READING® is designed to give every child a successful
reading experience. The grade levels are only guides; children will progress
through the steps at their own speed, developing confidence in their reading.
The F&P Text Level on the back cover serves as another tool to help you
choose the right book for your child.

Remember, a lifetime love of reading starts with a single step!

Visit us on the Web!
Seussville.com
randomhousekids.com
pbskids.org/catinthehat
treehousetv.com

Educators and librarians, for a variety of teaching tools, visit us at RHTeachersLibrarians.com

Library of Congress Cataloging-in-Publication Data
Names: Rabe, Tish, author. | Granleese, Patrick, screenwriter. | Brannon, Tom, illustrator.
Title: Have no fear! Halloween is here! / by Tish Rabe ; based on a television script by Patrick Granleese ; illustrated by Tom Brannon.
Description: First edition. | New York : Random House, 2016. | Series: Step into reading. Step 2
Identifiers: LCCN 2015021935| ISBN 978-1-101-93492-0 (trade pbk.) | ISBN 978-1-101-93493-7 (library bound hardcover) | ISBN 978-1-101-93494-4 (ebook)
Classification: LCC PZ8.3.R1145 Hav 2016 | DDC [E]—dc23
LC record available at http://lccn.loc.gov/2015021935

STEP INTO READING®

A SCIENCE READER

Have No Fear! Halloween Is Here!

by Tish Rabe

based on a television script by Patrick Granleese

illustrated by Tom Brannon

Random House 🏠 New York

"Nick," Sally said,
"I love Halloween!
And that's the *best* spider
I have ever seen!"

"Sally," said Nick, "what we need to do now is go find some costumes, but I don't know how."

5

"I do!" said the Cat.
"I know where to find
costumes for us
that are one of a kind.

We need to go now,
and we need to be quick."
"Yes—we need to be home
before dark," added Nick.

"Have no fear!" said the Cat.

"Come along. Follow me!

I know how to get there.

Come now, you will see."

Suddenly they heard
a chattering sound.
Everyone stopped.
They looked all around.

"That sound," Nick said,
"it came from in there.
Is it a monster?
A tiger? A bear?"

Then something flew out.
They all jumped a mile!
"Say, I *know* that bat,"
the Cat said with a smile.

"Sally and Nick,
meet my friend Batty Bat."
Batty flew down,
and he said, "Hello, Cat!"

13

"Batty," the Cat said,
"and other bats I have known
often chatter at dusk
before they leave home.

Bats are mammals that fly.
They like insects to eat.
Bats sleep during the day—
they hang by their feet!"

"We are here," Sally said,
"to find costumes today."
"Follow me!" Batty said.
"Flying is the best way."

So they started to fly,

but they saw a bright flash.

"Cat!" Sally said.

"Are we going to crash?"

"We are not," said the Cat.
"There is nothing to fear.
That is only some lightning.
It is far, far from here.

In fact, we have made it!
Look there, up ahead.
We are going to that
spooky house," the Cat said.

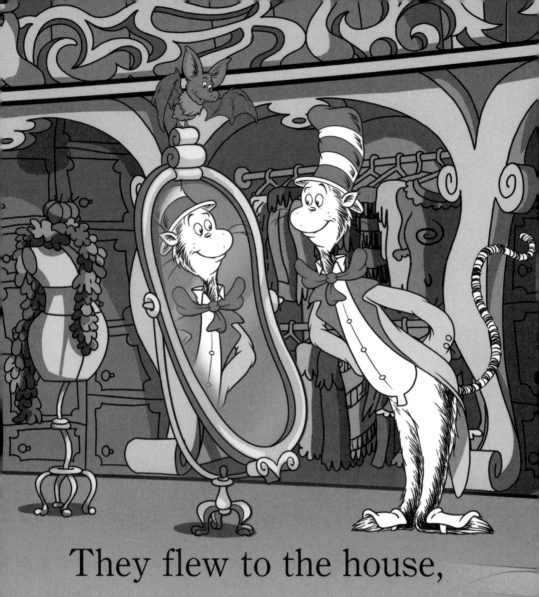

They flew to the house,
and each one got to pick
their favorite costume.
"We did it!" said Nick.

"These are the best costumes
we have ever seen!
Now we are ready. . . .

"Happy Halloween!"